MIND THE GAP!

Introduction

Compared with the main line railways of Britain, the London Underground receives the least attention from those who have an interest in railways. Maybe this is due to the fact that multiple unit trains dominate the system, and locomotive action is rare (though certainly not non-existent), or maybe it is just because the London Underground does what it does best day in, day out, and is very much taken for granted. This is certainly the case with most of the people who use it, who rarely look up from their newspapers to look at the train they are riding on, the architecture of the station they are passing through, or the complexity of the system over which they are travelling. The only time the majority of commuters ever look up and take notice is when something goes wrong, and then being delayed or not having a train on which to travel is a major problem in a city which is constantly on the move and nearly always in a hurry. London depends on the Underground to keep its people moving freely, and the system has had to adapt and change throughout its history to meet the current needs of the commuter. This has led to a lot of recent changes, and with the system now celebrating its 150th year, there are new trains being introduced, new lines and stations being built and old stations refurbished and modernised. There are many changes for an enthusiast photographer to capture.

In the past it was difficult to capture quality photographs of Underground trains running beneath the ground in their natural habitat. In 1992 I made a visit to London to record the 1962 stock on the Central Line before it was replaced with the then new 1992 stock trains. Armed with a roll of 1000asa slide film, I came away with a set of photos which are very grainy, under-exposed, and lack detail, some of which are also slightly blurred. In recent years the development of digital cameras and advanced digital photo processing techniques has made it possible to photograph the London Underground both above and below ground. Rather than carrying two different speeds of film, it is now just a case of adjusting the ISO setting on the camera. While the higher ISO settings enable good quality pictures to be taken underground, it must not be forgotten that most of the system actually runs above ground and there are some superb locations for capturing trains in urban landscapes. It has therefore been possible for me to record the current scene on the Underground in pictorial form, and that is what this book aims to portray. While the captions contain many historical and technical facts, it is not the intention of this book to be a complete history or technical book about the Underground. This is the London Underground today and over the past few years in pictorial form. The old trains being replaced, the new trains being introduced, the lines, the stations, all presented in full colour as a record of the London Underground as it celebrates its 150th year. Enjoy the book.

Jason Cross
Leicester, January 2013.

Above: A collector shoe flashes as a train of A stock departs from Harrow on the Hill.

Front cover: The new order on the sub-surface lines, the S stock trains. Built by Bombardier in Derby, these will eventually replace all trains on the Metropolitan, Hammersmith & City, Circle and District Lines. This is a Metropolitan example passing through West Hampstead with a train for Baker Street on the 26th May 2012.

Back cover: Replaced on Victoria Line services by new trains of 2009 stock, the 1967 stock last saw use in passenger service at the end of June 2011. Only a few vehicles now remain in departmental use. This is a train of the now replaced stock arriving at the Victoria's southern terminus at Brixton on the 21st August 2010.

All rights reserved. No part of this book may be reproduced or transmitted in any form or by any means, electronic or mechanical, including photocopying, scanning, recording or by any information storage and retrieval system, without written permission from the publisher.
Published by Videoscene, PO Box 243, Lytham St. Annes. FY8 9DE

On the Surface or Down the Tube?

Despite the system being generally known as 'the tube', not all of the London Underground lines are tube lines. When the first underground lines were built, they were constructed using the 'cut and cover' method. This involved digging a trench on the surface, building retaining walls along each side of the trench, laying the railway tracks in the bottom and then covering the trench over again. Not surprisingly, this was very disruptive and expensive. Some later lines were built by boring deep level tube tunnels, which could be built while life carried on as normal on the surface. The diameter of the tunnels determines the size of the trains and the deep level tube tunnels were smaller in diameter than those built by the cut and cover method, and therefore the trains that operate on them are smaller and are known as 'tube stock'. The larger trains which operate on the lines built by the cut and cover method are known as surface stock and are roughly the same size as trains which operate on the national railway network. This definition between the two types of trains is somewhat blurred by Transport for London themselves, who insist on calling the whole of the London Underground network by its affectionate name of 'the tube'.

Anyone who does not know that there are two sizes of rolling stock should take a look at this photograph as it clearly shows the difference. The train on the left is 1996 stock, working a Jubilee Line service for Stratford and is shown arriving at Kilburn station. The Jubilee is a deep level tube line and is operated by a fleet of 1996 stock trains built to tube size. Beyond Finchley Road station, this train will descend into tube tunnel for the journey under Central London.

The train on the right is surface stock and is visibly taller than the train on the left. This is Metropolitan Line A stock which is passing through Kilburn on the fast line with a service bound for Aldgate. The photo was taken on the 26th November 2011.

BAKERLOO LINE →

The Bakerloo is a deep level tube line which started life as the Baker Street & Waterloo Railway, opening between Baker Street and Kennington Road (now called Lambeth North) in March 1906. Extension to the current southern terminus at Elephant & Castle followed in August of the same year. In 1915, the line was extended northwards to Queens Park where the Bakerloo joined the London & North Western Railway's Watford DC lines with the tube trains running through to Watford Junction. Gradually, the Bakerloo services to Watford Junction were reduced and then withdrawn in 1982 with services cut back to Stonebridge Park. From 1984, Bakerloo trains were re-introduced north of Stonebridge Park again, but only as far north as Harrow & Wealdstone.

In 1939, a new section of tube tunnel opened to Finchley Road, branching off the existing Bakerloo Line at Baker Street. This allowed Bakerloo trains to run through to the Metropolitan Railway's Stanmore branch. From the 20th November 1939 the Stanmore branch was taken over by the Bakerloo to help ease congestion on the Metropolitan's main line into London. Further congestion problems, caused in the main by the two tracks of the Watford branch meeting the two tracks of the Stanmore branch at Baker Street where there were only three platforms, led to the construction of a fourth platform at Baker Street as part of a new tunnel section from there to Charing Cross. This became the Jubilee Line, and the Stanmore branch was transferred from the Bakerloo to the Jubilee on the 1st May 1979.

The Elephant & Castle to Harrow & Wealdstone route remains the extent of Bakerloo operations today. This is a route length of 14.4 miles, the first 6.75 miles of which (as far as Queens Park) are in tube tunnel. The line is currently operated by a fleet of Metropolitan-Cammell built 1972 MkII stock trains, which, following the withdrawal of the similar 1967 stock from the Victoria Line in 2011, are now the oldest tube trains in service on the London Underground.

Above: A smart looking train of 1972 MkII stock passes a not so smart looking retaining wall as it leaves Kensal Green with an Elephant & Castle bound Bakerloo service on the 19th March 2011. Sadly, it is often the trains which are the targeted victims of the graffiti artists! The 1972 MkII stock has been the mainstay of Bakerloo services since the 1980s and will most likely be the next type to be replaced when the Bakerloo Line is upgraded. They should however see out the 150th anniversary of the Underground and possibly a few more years after that.

On the 26th November 2011 and with driving motor 3233 leading, a train of 1972 MkII stock arrives at Elephant & Castle with a service from the north. Judging by the dot matrix indicator, this train will be leaving again in one minute with a service for Queens Park. Elephant & Castle is the southern terminus of the Bakerloo, and there is an interchange here with the Northern Line's City branch. Although all Bakerloo trains terminate here, the running tunnels do continue for a short distance beyond the platforms and there is room to stable up to four trains. There have been plans to extend the Bakerloo to Camberwell, but so far these have come to nothing.

Above: Charing Cross station was originally called Trafalgar Square when it was opened in 1906. Along with the nearby Strand station on the Northern Line, it was renamed to Charing Cross in 1979 when the new Jubilee Line terminus was opened. Advertising is a vital source of revenue for the London Underground, and advert posters inside trains, on escalators and on tunnel walls opposite the platforms are common. A recent innovation is the use of moving pictures to advertise. In this view, a digital projector can be clearly seen suspended from the tunnel roof. This projects TV style adverts onto the white screen on the tunnel wall. No image is being projected in this view however, as the projector will automatically switch off when a train enters the station. On the 19th February 2011, an Elephant & Castle to Queens Park service arrives with 3542 at the front.

Below: A very unusual layout exists at Piccadilly Circus on the Bakerloo. A trailing crossover occupies part of the station tunnel giving an open vista where trains travelling in both directions can be seen passing each other inside the same tunnel. In this view taken on the 26th November 2011, the southbound train on the left with 3549 at the rear is working a Queens Park to Elephant & Castle service, while heading north is 3565 with an Elephant & Castle to Queens Park working. The Bakerloo interchanges at Piccadilly Circus with the Piccadilly Line, and although the station was served first by the Bakerloo in March 1906, the station was also served by Piccadilly trains less than a year later in December 1906.

Above: One of the quietest stations in Central London is Regents Park. Here we see a southbound Bakerloo train destined for Elephant & Castle entering the station on the 26th November 2011. Roughly 3 million passengers a year start or finish their journeys here. Contrast that with the next station south of here, Oxford Circus, where the Bakerloo interchanges with two other tube lines, the Central and the Victoria, and this station sees roughly 70 million passengers per annum starting or ending their journeys there.

Below: 3541 leads an Elephant & Castle to Queens Park service into Marylebone on the 21st August 2010. Opened on the 27th March 1907, Marylebone tube station was originally called 'Great Central' after the name of the railway company which owned the main line railway terminus it serves. The platforms still display this name in the wall tiling (though not visible in this photograph). The station was renamed Marylebone on the 15th April 1917.

An Elephant & Castle to Queens Park service arrives at Maida Vale on the 26th November 2011. When opened, the Baker Street & Waterloo Railway built its platforms to a length of 288 feet. This was deemed inadequate and as part of the 1930s New Works Programme, the Bakerloo platforms were extended to 350 feet. Where the platforms have been lengthened, the size of the overall bore of the extended section is larger. This is clearly visible alongside the front cab of the train in this photograph. This station opened on the 31st January 1915 as part of the Baker Street & Waterloo's Paddington to Queens Park extension.

After a journey of 6.75 miles in tube tunnel, the Bakerloo emerges into daylight at Queens Park. On the far right of the picture can be seen the tracks of the West Coast Main Line in and out of London Euston. The Bakerloo tracks rise up between the northbound and southbound Watford DC lines, the southbound track being obscured by fencing between the retaining wall and the carriage shed. It will be noted that the northbound Watford DC line has the standard London Underground centre conductor rail in place (the southbound track does too) even though this is not part of the Bakerloo Line. This is to allow Bakerloo trains to run to and from Kilburn High Road to reverse should the need arise. The carriage shed in the centre of the picture is known as Queens Park South Carriage Shed and is used to stable trains overnight. Here a train of 1972 MkII stock with 3567 at the rear is descending into the tube tunnel with a Queens Park to Elephant & Castle service, while a northbound train is waiting at the signal at the exit of the tunnel, probably waiting while a Queens Park reverser clears the platform ahead. 19th March 2011.

This is Kilburn High Road, one stop south of Queens Park on the Watford DC Line towards Euston. It is not part of the Bakerloo Line and is actually part of Network Rail, but it does see the occasional visit from Bakerloo trains. In the event that a train arriving at Queens Park from the north needs to reverse, the train will run empty to Kilburn High Road and make use of the crossover at the north end of the station. This photograph, taken on the 11th March 2012, was taken while weekend engineering works had closed the Bakerloo south of Queens Park, and a shuttle service was operating between Harrow & Wealdstone and Queens Park. Trains used the outer platforms at Queens Park normally used by London Overground (Watford DC Line) services, and then ran to Kilburn High Road to reverse. The trains had to run out of service south of Queens Park as the platforms at Kilburn High Road are built to full height and the step up from tube stock is deemed to be too great. It will be noted that the left hand track also has the LUL centre conductor rail in place, this remains from the days when the crossover was at the south of the station. It is rare to see this move taking place in daylight, but a handful of Bakerloo trains are booked to reverse here during the night to keep the centre conductor rail free from rust.

An unusual layout exists at Queens Park station. At the north end of the platforms is Queens Park Carriage Shed, which consists of four roads. By night, all roads are used for the stabling of trains, but by day, the shed takes on a different role. Trains which terminate at Queens Park from the south run empty into either roads 22 or 23 where the driver will change ends before the train re-emerges and enters the platform to form another southbound train. Trains which continue north of Queens Park do so by running through the shed on road 21, while trains in the opposite direction run through road 24. Here we see a Harrow & Wealdstone to Elephant & Castle service passing through road 24 and entering the station on the 10th July 2010. This is the only location on the London Underground where passengers can experience passing through a carriage shed.

The delightful Kensal Green station is shared between London Overground services and London Underground Bakerloo Line services. Like all of the stations north of Queens Park, the platforms are built at a compromise height so that the step up from tube stock is roughly equal to the step down from mainline stock. Although Bakerloo services had started running north of Queens Park to Willesden Junction in May 1915, Kensal Green station was opened later and trains did not call here until October 1916. Here we see a Bakerloo Line train of 1972 MkII stock led by 3238 emerging from the 317 yard long Kensal Green tunnel into the station with a service for Elephant & Castle on the 10th July 2010.

A footbridge which crosses the railway just to the north of South Kenton station, taking pedestrians from Conway Gardens into Northwick Park. It is a very busy location for rail traffic and a very popular spot for railway enthusiasts. In this view, taken on the 24th March 2012, a Bakerloo Line train of 1972 MkII stock is heading south with a Harrow & Wealdstone to Elephant & Castle service and is about to slow for the South Kenton stop. The two left hand tracks carry both the London Overground Watford DC and Bakerloo Line trains. To the right of these are the four tracks of the West Coast Main Line, which are kept busy with a mix of local passenger, long distance passenger and freight workings. In the background can be seen the overbridge which not only carries the tracks of the Metropolitan Line, but also the Network Rail line, currently operated by Chiltern Railways from Marylebone to Aylesbury.

CENTRAL LINE →

The Central Line crosses London on an east to west axis and runs from Epping in the east to Ealing Broadway and West Ruislip in the west. There is also a loop which goes north out of Woodford, via Chigwell, Hainault and Newbury Park to rejoin the main line again three stops south of Woodford at Leytonstone.

The 'Twopenny Tube' as the Central Line was once affectionately known (as it charged a flat fare of two pence), was publicly opened as the Central London Railway between Shepherd's Bush and Bank in July 1900. The line has been extended several times in its lifetime. First of all was in 1908 when it was continued westwards from Shepherd's Bush on a loop to Wood Lane to serve the Franco-British Exhibition. Four years later in 1912, the east end of the line was extended to Liverpool Street to serve the Great Eastern Railway's main line railway terminus. 1920 saw another extension, this time in conjunction with the Great Western Railway's 'Ealing & Shepherd's Bush Railway' to Ealing Broadway. CLR trains heading towards Ealing Broadway emerged from the Wood Lane loop on the right hand side, and this resulted in a flyover being built adjacent to Wormwood Scrubs prison to revert the tracks back to left hand running, an arrangement which still exists to this day.

The London Passenger Transport Board's 1935 'New Works Programme' included plans for extensions to both ends of the Central Line. At the east end, the line would be continued to Epping over former Eastern Counties Railway (later GER, LNER and BR) tracks, with a section of new tube tunnel linking Leytonstone with Newbury Park to form a loop via Hainault and Chigwell to join the Epping line in the southbound direction at Woodford. The outbreak of World War II delayed these plans, with the first section from Liverpool Street to Stratford not opening until December 1946. Opening to Woodford and Newbury Park followed in 1947, with the loop via Chigwell in 1948 and the remaining section north from Woodford to Epping in 1949. The Central Line then took over the Epping to Ongar line from British Railways in 1957, but this section later closed in September 1994, and is now a preserved railway. At the west end of the line an extension to West Ruislip was built which diverged from the Ealing Broadway line at North Acton. This line opened to Greenford in 1947 and then to West Ruislip in 1948.

Today a fleet of 1992 stock trains built by ABB Transportation (now Bombardier) and introduced to the line from 1993 onwards work the line. The Central Line operates using ATO (Automatic Train Operation) and ATP (Automatic Train Protection). This allows the trains to work automatically with the ATO driving the train and the ATP picking up codes in the track to detect target speeds. This method of operation also allows for quick running and the Central Line is considered to be the fastest of the tube lines with a top speed approaching 70mph.

Above: Here a train of 1992 stock approaches South Woodford with a westbound service on the 15th October 2011.

The 1992 stock trains used on the Central Line were built by ABB Transportation in Derby. They first entered service on the Central in 1993 to replace the 1962 stock which had operated on the line since the early 1960s. The last train of 1962 stock ran in 1995 and the 1992 stock has dominated Central Line services ever since. They have not been trouble free however, and in January 2003 a westbound train approaching Chancery Lane was derailed by a traction motor becoming detached. The cause was found to be faulty bolts and the entire 1992 stock fleet was withdrawn to have these replaced. Trains were gradually put back into service, but it took nearly 6 months for full operation to be restored. Thankfully, since this event, the 1992 stock has settled down to give good reliable service.

Above: With the use of a wide angle lens and a bit of lucky timing, it has been possible to capture two 1992 stock tube trains in the open vista that exists at the east end of Shepherd's Bush station. The train on the left is westbound to White City, while the train on the right is eastbound to Hainault via Woodford. Opened on the 30th July 1900, Shepherd's Bush was the original western terminus of the Central London Railway. The station became a through station in 1908 when the Wood Lane loop was opened.

Below: The sub surface Metropolitan Railway first reached Notting Hill Gate in October 1868, with the deep level Central London Railway station opening in 1900. However, both railways had separate entrances for their stations and it was not until 1959 that the two stations were linked together. Since then there has been a proper interchange facility between the former MR platforms, which are now part of the Circle and District Lines, and the CLR platforms which are now part of the Central Line. When built, the CLR tube stations were very sparsely decorated with plain white tiling on the walls. Notting Hill Gate station retains much of this appearance, although the tiles are not the original ones. Here we see a westbound train for Ealing Broadway arriving at the station on the 21st January 2012.

An Epping bound train of 1992 stock arrives at Bethnal Green on the 15th October 2011. Sadly a very tragic event took place here during the war that resulted in a great loss of life. Although the Central Line's eastern extension did not open until after the war, the tunnels were largely complete when war broke out. Many tube stations were used as air raid shelters during the German bombing of London, and the incomplete Bethnal Green station was no exception. On the evening of the 3rd March 1943, a new type of anti-aircraft rocket was launched from the nearby Victoria Park, and the unfamiliar noise of the explosion caused people to panic and run to Bethnal Green station to take shelter. A person, believed to be a lady carrying a child, tripped and fell on the stairs, and within a very short time approximately 300 people were crushed into the small stairwell. A total of 173 people were killed, mainly through suffocation. The Bethnal Green disaster was the largest loss of civilian life due to a single incident during World War II. A very sad event, and one which few of those who pass through Bethnal Green are probably aware.

Leytonstone is a junction on the Central Line where the south end of the Hainault loop joins the main route of the Central Line from Epping. Although the Central Line reached here in May 1947, the railway through this station actually pre-dates the entire London Underground as it was opened by the Eastern Counties Railway back in August 1856, later becoming part of the Great Eastern Railway and then part of the London & North Eastern Railway. The New Works Programme Central Line extension saw the LNER tracks taken over by London Transport to become a part of the Central Line. A new section of tube line was also built which branches off here for Newbury Park, and in this view taken on the 15th October 2011, a train for Hainault is beginning its descent into the tube for the run through Wanstead, Gants Hill and Newbury Park to Hainault. Trains for Epping continue straight on here, and a train from Epping can just be seen approaching in the distance.

Above: The new section of tube tunnel between Leytonstone and Newbury Park was under construction when the Second World War broke out. The tunnels themselves were largely complete, although none of the track and signalling had been installed and the stations had not been fitted out when work stopped due to the war. In 1942, the yet to be used tunnels were adapted by the Plessey Company into a long wartime production factory to manufacture aircraft components. Protected from the bombing above ground, the top-secret factory employed more than 2000 people and even had a narrow gauge railway to transport materials and components between the various workstations. This is Wanstead station on the 21st August 2010 with a westbound train arriving. It is hard to believe that this station area was once a hive of activity with the assembly lines for the various aircraft parts located here.

Below: Another station that was part of the underground factory was Gants Hill, and this location was used as the coil winding shop. After the end of the war, work resumed on extending the Central Line, and the new tube tunnel section was completed and eventually opened on the 14th December 1947. Today the station is served by a frequent service with trains usually running to and from either Newbury Park, Hainault or Woodford (via Hainault). This view shows a train of 1992 stock arriving with a train for Hainault on the 21st August 2010.

Above: Gants Hill station was designed by London Transport architect Charles Holden. During the design of Gants Hill, Holden was influenced by stations on the Moscow Metro, and incorporated a Moscow style barrel vaulted roof over the concourse between the eastbound and westbound platforms. It is very different to anything else on the Underground and is one of many legacies left behind by this great architect. The photo shows the station as it appears today, pretty much how Holden designed it, and well looked after and cared for.

Below: After travelling from Leytonstone through the tube tunnel stations of Wanstead, Redbridge and Gants Hill, the line emerges into daylight at Newbury Park where the line joins the formation of the former Ilford to Woodford line opened by the Great Eastern Railway in May 1903. This station saw its first tube trains at the same time as the tube tunnel section from Leytonstone opened in December 1947. However, trains terminated here and then ran empty from here to the new depot at Hainault. Passenger services through to Hainault did not commence until the 31st May 1948. Here we see a train of 1992 stock arriving with a Hainault to Ealing Broadway service on the 19th November 2011. Some trains still terminate at Newbury Park using the centre reversing track which can be seen to the left of the train.

JUBILEE LINE →

Construction work began in 1971 on a new section of tube tunnel between Baker Street and Charing Cross. This was to have been called the Fleet Line, but as it was scheduled to open in 1977, the year of Her Majesty Queen Elizabeth II's Silver Jubilee, it was renamed the Jubilee Line. In the event, the new line did not open until 1979, and as well as the new section between Baker Street and Charing Cross, the Jubilee also took over the Stanmore branch from the Bakerloo. The Jubilee operated over this route until 1999 when the new Jubilee Line Extension (JLE) to Stratford was opened. This new line branched off of the existing Jubilee Line just after Green Park station, causing the terminus at Charing Cross to close, although it is still retained for non passenger carrying reversing moves should the need arise for trains to terminate at Green Park.

When the Jubilee first operated in 1979, it was worked by trains of 1972 MkII stock (now on the Bakerloo), and these were subsequently replaced by newly built trains of 1983 stock. These were short lived as their single leaf passenger doors caused delays during station stops, and when the JLE was built, a new fleet of 1996 stock trains were ordered from Alsthom and the 1983 stock was withdrawn. Today the line runs from Stratford to Stanmore and is worked by the 1996 stock trains. Since June 2011, these trains have operated in automatic mode.

Above: Stanmore, northern terminus of the Jubilee Line with all three platforms occupied. The platform on the right of the picture is newly built and was vital in allowing the train frequency to be increased when the line was re-signalled and switched over to automatic operation. The new platform opened in July 2011 and became platform 3. Adding the new platform on this side of the station means that it is actually alongside platform 1, so the platform numbers are out of sequence being numbered 3, 1, 2 from right to left. This picture was taken on the 19th November 2011.

Above: The first station south of the Stanmore terminus is Canons Park, and here we see a 1996 stock train led by 96009 approaching the station on the 16th September 2007. This photograph was taken from the front cab of a train of 1938 tube stock which was working a railtour from Charing Cross to Stanmore. Since the Jubilee Line switched over to automatic train operation in 2011, it is now no longer possible to operate heritage trains over this line as only the 1996 tube stock is compatible with the new signalling system. The colour light signal on the left of the picture has also been made redundant by the new signalling system.

Below: A northbound Jubilee train departs from Kingsbury station with a service for Stanmore on the 19th June 2011. Kingsbury station was opened as part of the Metropolitan Railway's Stanmore branch in December 1932. Since the line was transferred to the Bakerloo in 1939, the Stanmore Branch has been operated by tube size stock, but all the overbridges show their MR parentage as they are still high enough to accommodate sub surface size stock.

A train of 1996 stock led by driving motor 96084 approaches Neasden station while working a Stanmore bound service on the 19th June 2011. The blue marker boards seen alongside the train are standard on the Underground and tell the driver how many carriages of the train are off the platform. Should the passenger alarm be triggered while departing from the station, the driver will only stop the train if one or more carriages are still in the platform, otherwise the train must continue to the next station.

The bridge above the rear of the train carries the Network Rail line between Cricklewood and Acton and is mainly used by freight traffic.

In 2012, Her Majesty Queen Elizabeth II celebrated her Diamond Jubilee, and to celebrate this, London Underground applied a special livery to two trains of 1996 tube stock on the Jubilee Line. The special livery was applied using vinyls and consisted of a large section of the Union flag on the side of each carriage, as well as Diamond Jubilee logos on the carriage sides and the cab ends. One of the trains is seen slowing for the Willesden Green stop with a Stratford to Stanmore service on the 26th May 2012. In the background, a train of S stock can also be seen passing non stop through Willesden Green station. Opened by the Metropolitan Railway in 1879, the station building still proudly displays the name 'Metropolitan Railway'. Today, Willesden Green is only served by trains on the Jubilee Line, although the platforms on the Metropolitan tracks are still intact and can be used if necessary. This only tends to occur if the Jubilee Line is closed or suspended while the Metropolitan is still running.

Looking towards the centre of London from the Mapesbury Road Bridge, we see a northbound Jubilee Line train departing from Kilburn station. This photograph shows the layout of Kilburn station to good effect with the island platform serving the northbound and southbound Jubilee Lines, and the northbound and southbound Metropolitan Lines on the outside of the two Jubilee tracks. A northbound train of Metropolitan Line A stock can be seen passing Kilburn station in the distance. The two tracks far right are the Network Rail tracks into Marylebone.

The photograph was taken on the 26th June 2011, and it will be noticed that the conductor rails over which the train is passing are rusty. This was the day when the new Thales S40 moving block signalling system was switched on and the train pictured was one of the first northbound trains to run and test the system. Later the same day, normal passenger services resumed with trains operating in automatic mode.

Above: A Stanmore to Stratford service arrives at Swiss Cottage on the 13th February 2010. This section of tunnel between Finchley Road and Baker Street started life as part of the Bakerloo Line, opening to passengers on the 20th November 1939, eventually replacing the adjacent Swiss Cottage station on the Metropolitan Line which was closed in August 1940. Despite later becoming part of the new Jubilee Line in 1979, the station still remains little changed from when it opened in 1939.

Below: The Jubilee Line was extended to Stratford in the 1990s and opened in stages between the summer and December of 1999. The new tube tunnel section south of Green Park has stations built with platform edge doors which only open when a train has stopped with its doors in line with the doors on the platform edge. This makes it almost impossible to photograph trains on this section of line. The last part of the extension is above ground though and there are no platform edge doors on this section. This is the Stratford terminus of the line on the 16th August 2008. The Jubilee platforms here are separate to the existing station and are alongside the former North London Line platforms which are now used by the Docklands Light Railway.

NORTHERN LINE →

The Northern Line is the only tube line to have two routes through the centre of London. It was also the first underground line to be constructed in deep level tubes when its first section was opened by the City & South London Railway in November 1890 between Stockwell and King William Street. Further extensions saw this line running from Clapham Common to Euston by 1907. Also in this year, the Charing Cross, Euston & Hampstead Railway (the Hampstead Tube) opened between Charing Cross and Camden Town where the line split to go to Highgate (now Archway) and Golders Green. In the 1920s, the two companies lines were brought together and also extended northwards from Golders Green to Edgware and southward to Morden. Further extension northwards took place in the late 1930s with the line to High Barnet and a branch to Mill Hill East opening over former Great Northern Railway tracks. High Barnet opened to tube trains in April 1940, with the Mill Hill East branch following in May 1941.

No further expansion of the Northern Line has taken place since, so today the line from High Barnet and the Mill Hill East branch meet the Edgware branch at Camden Town, where the line splits again with one line running via Bank, and the other running via Charing Cross.

Both come together again at Kennington for the run to Morden. Train services are operated by a fleet of 1995 stock trains built by Alsthom and introduced to the line between 1998 and 2001.

Externally, the 1995 stock used on the Northern is almost identical to the 1996 stock used on the Jubilee Line, and in fact both types were built alongside one another at Alsthom in Birmingham. The only reason they have been designated as 1995 and 1996 stock is to differentiate between the two types and if you look at the step plates in the passenger entrance doors of the 1995 stock, they do in fact state 1996. Beneath the skin, the two train types are very different, with the 1995 stock having a more up to date control system than the 1996 stock. This is very apparent when the two trains are heard, the 1996 stock making a very distinctive constantly changing whining noise, whereas the 1995 stock is much quieter.

Above: In this view taken on the 26th November 2011, a southbound train heading for Morden calls at Borough on the Bank branch.

Above: The High Barnet branch of the Northern runs over a line that was built by the Great Northern Railway (GNR), and was latterly operated by the London & North Eastern Railway (LNER) until taken over by the London Passenger Transport Board. The first LPTB Northern Line trains ran in April 1940. Even today, there are many signs to indicate the history of this line. Many stations still retain many of their Great Northern Railway buildings, such as here at Totteridge & Whetstone. In this scene, passengers make their way towards the exit as a High Barnet bound train departs on the 23rd June 2012.

Below: Woodside Park station was opened as Torrington Park on the 1st April 1872 by the Great Northern Railway. Just one month later, it was renamed Torrington Park, Woodside, and was then renamed again in May 1882 to its current name of Woodside Park. Sitting at the north end of the station is a remarkable survivor, a Great Northern Railway signalbox. The box has not signalled a train for many years, and remarkably, well into the 21st century, there were actually two GNR boxes here, the second being roughly level with the far end of the train. Along with High Barnet, Finchley Central, East Finchley and Totteridge & Whetstone, Woodside Park retained a goods yard long after the line was transferred over to tube operation. Freight trains were operated by the LNER and latterly BR and ran until 1962. The goods yard here was behind the tree on the right of the picture in what is now the station car park.

All other photographs in this book of tube trains in underground tube stations are taken while the train is still moving. This is due to the fact that when a train calls at a tube station, it fills the length of the platform. One exception is Highgate on the Northern Line, where unusually the platforms are longer than the trains which serve them. In an attempt to ease overcrowding on the Northern in the 1930s, some 9 car trains were introduced, the standard train on the Northern being 7 cars. The platforms at Highgate and Golders Green were made long enough to accept all 9 cars, and the rear two cars were used exclusively by passengers travelling to and from Tottenham Court Road. At each station, the two extra cars would remain in the tunnels, and only at Tottenham Court Road station would they be pulled forward into the platform. Here we see a train of 1995 stock calling at Highgate on the 23rd June 2012 with a service for High Barnet. The photo was taken just after the doors of the train closed, but before the train started moving.

Passengers wait patiently for a train of 1995 stock to draw to a halt at Elephant & Castle on the Bank branch of the Northern Line with a service for Morden on the 26th November 2011. Opened in December 1890, Elephant & Castle was one of six stations served by the world's first deep level tube railway, the City & South London Railway between King William Street and Stockwell. The station was served exclusively by the CSLR until 1906 when the Baker Street & Waterloo Railway (now the Bakerloo Line) opened and the Northern and Bakerloo have formed an interchange here ever since. Ironically, Northern Line trains travelling to Morden are heading for the southernmost point on the entire Underground network.

Above: A station layout favoured by the City & South London Railway tube stations was a central island platform serving two tracks within one tunnel. Most of these have been rebuilt, the most recent being at Angel where a new station tunnel was bored and the northbound line diverted through it, leaving the original station bore with just the one track and an unusually wide platform. There is also evidence of this at Euston on the Bank branch of the Northern, where what is now the southbound tunnel used to house both the northbound and southbound tracks. The northbound track at Euston was diverted as part of a major rebuild to accommodate the then new Victoria Line in the 1960s. Amazingly though, there are two stations which still retain the two tracks inside one tunnel, and these are Clapham Common and Clapham North. This is 21st June 2009, with a Morden to High Barnet via Bank service arriving at Clapham North. It is worth noting that both of these stations are south of Kennington where the Bank and the Charing Cross branches of the Northern split, so northbound trains will at this point show their route through London as well as their destination on the front.

Below: Same day at Clapham Common station with a Morden bound train arriving on the right of the picture, and a Morden to Edgware via Bank service departing on the left.

PICCADILLY LINE →

Opened by the Great Northern, Piccadilly & Brompton Railway in 1906 between Finsbury Park and Hammersmith, the Piccadilly Line as it is now known is a deep level tube line. Further extension of the route came in the 1930s with the current northern terminus at Cockfosters being reached in July 1933. At the west end of the line, the Piccadilly was extended to Uxbridge and Hounslow West over tracks formerly operated by the District Railway. Further extension occurred in the late 1970s when a new line was opened beyond Hounslow West to serve Heathrow Airport Terminals 1, 2 and 3 (opened as Heathrow Central). This extension has been further enhanced as the airport has expanded with a terminal loop serving Terminal 4 opening in April 1986, and a spur to Terminal 5 opening in March 2008.

Built to coincide with the opening of the Heathrow extension, the 1973 stock which operates the line today was built with airport traffic in mind and has more luggage space and less seating as a consequence. The line today runs from Cockfosters in the north of the capital, through the centre of London to Acton Town where the route splits with the Uxbridge line and the Heathrow Airport branch splitting to the west of the station.

Above: The newest station on the Piccadilly Line opened in March 2008 to serve the newly built Heathrow Airport Terminal 5. Unlike the Heathrow Terminals 1, 2 and 3 and Terminal 4 stations which are both served by a loop line, the Terminal 5 station is a terminus at the end of a stub which branches off the Heathrow loop just to the west of the Terminal 1, 2 and 3 station. Here we see a typical Piccadilly Line train formed of 1973 stock pulling into the arrivals only platform on the 19th June 2011. Trains from London arrive in this set down only platform, and then run empty into sidings to reverse before running into the opposite platform which is pick up only.

Opposite: Ealing Common is shared between the District Line's Ealing Broadway branch and the Piccadilly Line's Uxbridge branch. The two lines separate a short distance to the north of Ealing Common at Hangar Lane Junction where the District turns left into Ealing Broadway station. The Metropolitan District Railway opened the station as part of its Ealing Broadway extension from Turnham Green in 1879, with the line to South Harrow opening in 1903. The latter line was extended to join the Metropolitan Railway at Rayners Lane in 1910 thus enabling District Railway trains to run through to Uxbridge. In October 1933, the Uxbridge branch from Ealing Common was taken over by the Piccadilly, and this arrangement remains to this day. Here we see a Piccadilly line train of 1973 stock departing from Ealing Common with an early morning Rayners Lane to Acton Town service just as an Ealing Broadway bound District Line train arrives in the opposite direction. The photo was taken on the 21st January 2012.

Opposite: Ever since the Piccadilly Line took over the line north of Hangar Lane Junction to Rayners Lane from the District in 1933, tube trains have been a common sight running through to the terminus at Uxbridge. This view taken on the 26th June 2011 shows a Piccadilly Line train departing from Uxbridge with a service for Cockfosters. Uxbridge is also served by the sub surface trains of the Metropolitan Line, and several trains of the now withdrawn A stock can be seen in Uxbridge carriage sidings in the background. A partial closure of the Metropolitan Line meant that several trains were sitting spare in the sidings for the weekend. The original Uxbridge station was opened by the Metropolitan Railway in 1904, and was located on Belmont Road, roughly where the Sainsbury's supermarket is situated in the above photograph. This was closed on the 4th December 1938 to be replaced by the current terminus in the High Street on the same day.

Above: A train of 1973 tube stock arrives at Sudbury Town with a Rayners Lane to Cockfosters Piccadilly Line service on the 21st January 2012. The station buildings here are grade II listed and are a classic example of the 'brick box with concrete lid' architecture so typical of the work of Charles Holden who designed them. The interior of the station has been superbly restored, and while most commuters probably pass through it without taking too much notice, for anyone interested in architecture, the station is well worth a visit. As already mentioned, this section of railway was once a part of the District Railway, being taken over by the Piccadilly in 1932 as far as South Harrow and then through to Rayners Lane and over the Metropolitan to Uxbridge in 1933. Even to this day, the height of the platforms are still compatible with sub surface size trains, even though the line is only ever used by the tube trains of the Piccadilly.

A very busy scene at Acton Town on the 23rd June 2012. In the centre of the shot, a Piccadilly Line train of 1973 stock is taking the Heathrow branch with a service for Heathrow Terminal 5, while on the left of the shot, another train of 1973 stock is climbing up to pass over the top of the Heathrow branch with a Piccadilly Line service for Rayners Lane. On the right hand side is a train of District Line D stock with a service from Ealing Broadway.

When it was opened by the Metropolitan District Railway in 1879, Acton Town was known as Mill Hill Park and was renamed to Acton Town in 1910. The Piccadilly Line reached here in 1932 and has run alongside the District Line services here ever since. Train frequency is very high with Piccadilly trains running to and from the Uxbridge line or the Heathrow branch and District trains to and from Ealing Broadway, making photographs with one, two, three or even four trains in the shot fairly easy to obtain. The line branching off to the right under the second carriage of the D stock train is the exit road from Ealing Common depot.

Above: On the 7th March 2009, a train of 1973 stock passes non stop through Ravenscourt Park station and is heading towards the centre of London. The stretch of line between Acton Town and Hammersmith is unusual in that only District Line trains call at Chiswick Park, Turnham Green, Stamford Brook and Ravenscourt Park, while Piccadilly Line trains run non stop. The track layout along this stretch consists of the two fast tracks in the centre, with the slow lines on the outside. The slow lines are usually used by the District with the Piccadilly trains on the fast, but occasionally for operational reasons trains from both lines may run on either. Just to the east of Barons Court, the Piccadilly Line tracks burrow down into tube tunnel while the District tracks remain on the surface. There is the risk that a full size District Line train could be wrongly routed into the tube tunnel, and to prevent this there are three glass hoops suspended from a gantry between Hammersmith and Barons Court stations. Tube stock can pass underneath them, but a full size train would smash them, breaking a relay circuit and instantly shutting off the traction current.

Below: A Cockfosters bound train arrives at Hyde Park Corner on the 13th February 2010. The station here has no buildings above ground and is accessed from the pedestrian underpass which goes under the road junction here. When it was opened in December 1906 by the Great Northern, Piccadilly & Brompton Railway, it had a station building designed by Leslie Green. This building still exists, but is no longer used for its original purpose, having been taken out of use during the 1930s when the station was rebuilt. The building is easy to spot as it still has the distinctive dark red tiles so typical of a Leslie Green designed station.

VICTORIA LINE →

The Victoria Line was built to relieve congestion on other lines in the central area of London. Construction began in 1962 with the first section between Walthamstow Central and Highbury & Islington opening on the 1st September 1968. Opening as far as Warren Street took place later in 1968, and then on the 7th March 1969, the line between Walthamstow Central and Victoria was officially opened by Her Majesty Queen Elizabeth II. In 1967, approval was granted for a further extension southward from Victoria to Brixton. This was opened on the 23rd July 1971 and thus the full route of the line remains today as Walthamstow Central to Brixton.

Right from day one, the line has been worked automatically, with train operators working the passenger doors and then pressing two start buttons to start the train. If the line ahead is clear, the train sets off and stops at the next station without any further intervention. Train operators can drive the trains manually if needed and when running to and from the line's depot at Northumberland Park.

When opened, the line was operated by a fleet of 1967 stock trains built by Metropolitan-Cammell in Birmingham. These served the line for over 40 years before being replaced by new trains of 2009 stock built by Bombardier Transportation in Derby. The last train of 1967 stock ran on the 30th June 2011.

Following the withdrawal of the 1967 stock, the 2009 stock has now settled down to give good service on the Victoria Line. The trains are 1.6 inches wider, and 9.8 feet longer than the 1967 stock trains they have replaced. This gives them capacity to carry 19% more passengers than the older trains. They also accelerate faster and there are six more sets of 2009 stock than there were of the 1967 stock meaning a higher frequency of service can be provided.

Above: Here we see set 11067-11068 entering Warren Street with a Brixton bound service on the 23rd June 2012.

Opposite: The Victoria Line is not the most interesting line to photograph. The entire line from Walthamstow Central to Brixton is underground with only the line's depot at Northumberland Park being above ground, and most of the stations follow a very similar design. This is Blackhorse Road station which is one stop short of the northern terminus at Walthamstow Central, and here we see a Brixton to Walthamstow Central service entering the station on the 21st August 2010. Interchange is available here with the London Overground Gospel Oak to Barking service.

Opposite: The southern terminus of the Victoria Line is at Brixton and was opened on the 23rd July 1971 by Princess Alexandra. Trains which terminate here usually head straight back north, however the running tunnels continue south from here for a short distance where there is room to stable up to four trains beyond the platform ends. When this photograph was taken on the 15th February 2011, the 1967 stock trains had only a few more months left in traffic and more than half of the services on this day were in the hands of the new 2009 stock trains. By the end of June of that year, the entire service was being worked by the new trains, and the 1967 stock fleet had been sent away to the scrap yard. A train of the old stock is seen arriving at the southern terminus of the line at Brixton with a service from the north, probably from either Walthamstow Central or Seven Sisters.

Above: An interior view of 1967 stock trailer 4115 showing the longitudinal seating arrangement. There was also some transverse seating in other parts of the train. All of the 1967 stock underwent refurbishment at Rosyth Dockyard in the 1990s and part of the work included the fitting of grab poles in the line's colour of light blue.

Below: As the Victoria Line tube tunnels were built to a slightly larger overall diameter than other tube lines, when replacement trains were ordered, it was possible to take advantage of this and make the trains to a slightly larger overall size. This meant however, that when the 2009 stock was being delivered from Bombardier in Derby, it could not be delivered by rail, as this would have involved the trains gaining access to the Victoria via the Piccadilly at Finsbury Park, and the new trains would not fit in the tube tunnels of the Piccadilly. All vehicles were therefore delivered individually by road to Northumberland Park depot, and here we see trailer 13069 heading south at junction 23 of the M1 motorway near Loughborough in Leicestershire on the 10th April 2011. Likewise, should the trains need to leave the line in the future for heavy maintenance or refurbishment, they will only be able to do so by road. Ironically, as each train of 2009 stock entered service, a train of 1967 stock would be fitted with trip cocks and driven manually down to Acton for component recovery before being sent away by road for scrap.

When the Victoria Line was built in the 1960s, there were quite severe budget constraints and where possible costs were kept low. This is apparent in the width of the station platforms which are generally much narrower than on other lines. The Victoria has become far busier than predicted and is now the most heavily used line on the Underground in terms of average number of journeys per mile. At times, the narrow platforms can become dangerously overcrowded and it is quite common for some of the busier stations to close for short periods for safety reasons. The new 2009 stock trains can carry more people and run at closer intervals than the 1967 stock, and this helps to minimise the build up of waiting passengers at platform level. When built, the line was intended to relieve the pressure on other Underground lines and to provide as many interchanges with other Underground and British Rail lines as possible. In fact the only station on the Victoria Line that does not interchange with another railway line is Pimlico where we see a train of 2009 stock arriving on the 15th February 2011.

WATERLOO & CITY LINE →

The shortest line on the London Underground and with only two stations at Waterloo and at Bank, the Waterloo & City Line is a self-contained operation. It has only been a part of the London Underground since 1994, but its history stretches much further back. The line was opened as the Waterloo & City Railway in 1898 and at the time it was only the second electric tube railway after the City & South London Railway (now the Northern Line). Although the line was owned and operated by the L&SWR, it was run as a separate company until 1906 when it became a proper part of the L&SWR. In 1923, under the grouping of British railways, the line became part of the Southern Railway, and then when the railways were nationalised in 1948, it became part of British Railways Southern Region. It was run by BR up until privatisation with ownership being transferred from BR to London Underground from the 1st April 1994. The Waterloo & City's main purpose is to take City workers between Waterloo station and the financial district at Bank. For this reason, the line does not operate on Sundays and Bank Holidays.

The line is operated by a small fleet of 1992 stock trains, which are almost identical to those used on the Central Line. These were ordered by British Rail and were delivered in 1993 to replace the former Southern Railway stock that dated back to 1940 (British Rail class 487). The trains are housed in a small depot at Waterloo where most maintenance tasks are undertaken. Being totally separate to the rest of the Underground means that in the event of a train needing maintenance above that which can be carried out at Waterloo depot, they have to be craned out and taken away by road.

Above: Led by 65510, a train of 1992 stock arrives at Waterloo with a service from Bank on the 13th February 2010. This platform is only used for arriving trains, and once all the passengers have alighted, this train will draw forward into Waterloo depot, the driver will change ends and the train will move forward into the departure platform, which is situated behind the wall on the left. With a journey time of only around 4 minutes, there are no intermediate stations along the line. If you look closely at the platform edge, the old Network Southeast logos can still be seen partially obscured by the yellow line alongside the first carriage of the train.

METROPOLITAN LINE →

Having opened the first underground railway in the world in 1863, the Metropolitan Railway set about branching out towards the suburbs from Baker Street. Harrow was reached in 1880, followed by Rickmansworth in 1887, Chesham in 1889, and Aylesbury in 1892 where it joined the Aylesbury & Buckingham Railway to allow Metropolitan Railway trains to work through to Verney Junction, some 50 miles from the centre of London. Trains to Verney Junction were eventually withdrawn back to Aylesbury from 1936. The Uxbridge branch, which left the existing Metropolitan Railway line at Harrow, was opened in 1904 and this was followed in 1925 by the Watford branch which left the main route of the Metropolitan to the north of Moor Park station. In December 1932, the Metropolitan Railway opened a branch line from Wembley Park to Stanmore. With trains from Aylesbury, Chesham, Watford, Uxbridge and now Stanmore all trying to share the two-track section between Finchley Road and Baker Street, this section of line became congested. A new line was built in tube tunnel from Finchley Road to Baker Street to connect with the Bakerloo Line, and Stanmore trains were transferred over to the Bakerloo from the 20th November 1939.

The Metropolitan was only electrified as far as Rickmansworth, and any trains travelling through to locations north of here would be hauled by an electric locomotive as far as Rickmansworth where a steam loco would take over. The line north of Rickmansworth was eventually electrified in 1961, but only as far as Amersham, and Metropolitan Line services were then withdrawn north of Amersham.

The Cravens built A stock was introduced to coincide with the electrification to Amersham, and they were to take over all Metropolitan Line services from this time until they were eventually replaced by new 8-car S stock trains in 2012. The last train of A stock ran in normal passenger service on the 26th September, followed by a final railtour on the 29th September. Today the Metropolitan still operates to Uxbridge, Watford, Chesham and Amersham, with trains usually running through to either Baker Street or Aldgate. North of Harrow on the Hill on the Amersham line, the Metropolitan shares tracks with train services from London Marylebone to Aylesbury operated by Chiltern Trains, and any Network Rail train operating over this route must be fitted with trip cocks to be compatible with the London Underground signalling which is used on this stretch of line.

By the summer of 2012, it was pretty much game over for the A stock trains which had been the mainstay of Metropolitan Line services for over 50 years. Only a handful remained as spares in case there were a high number of S stock failures during the London Olympic Games. It is sad to see these trains withdrawn and sent away for scrap, but such is the price of progress, and the new S stock trains which replace them are very smart and should serve the Metropolitan well for many years to come. With the introduction of these trains across not just the Metropolitan, but also the Hammersmith & City, Circle and District Lines, there will, for the first time, be a standard train across all of the sub-surface lines.

Above: This view taken at Willesden Green in May 2012 shows the transition period when S stock and A stock could be seen operating side by side.

The current Hillingdon station on the Uxbridge line only dates back to 1994, but the Metropolitan Railway opened the first station here as long ago as 1904. The original station was roughly where the train is in the above photograph, but this was demolished to make way for the A40 Western Avenue over which the train is passing. This image was taken on the bright and sunny morning of the 19th of March 2011, driving motor 5223 leads the way over the A40 with an Uxbridge to Harrow on the Hill service. This was a Saturday morning, and a weekend line blockade was in force south of Harrow on the Hill meaning that all southbound trains terminated there with rail replacement buses taking passengers forward towards the city. A replacement bus service is not the ideal, but at least passengers from the Uxbridge area had the option of taking a Piccadilly Line train to Central London instead.

Much of London is still sleeping as the Underground begins to wake from its overnight slumber. This is 05:24 on the morning of the 21st January 2012, and the very first southbound Metropolitan Line train of the day is arriving at Rayners Lane. This is the 05:11 from Uxbridge, which under normal circumstances would go through to Aldgate, but on this day, the Metropolitan was partly closed due to engineering works, and all Metropolitan Line trains were terminating at Harrow on the Hill. 2012 was to be the last year of the A stock trains in normal passenger service, and they will be sorely missed by some commuters. They were designed to be an outer suburban train with plenty of large comfortable transverse seats and not much room for standing passengers. A feature not seen in any Underground trains in recent times are the overhead luggage racks that these trains were fitted with right until the end. By comparison, the S stock trains which have replaced them have fewer seats and more room for standing passengers and some regular commuters view them as a retrograde step. However, the new trains are designed to be easier for anyone with a disability to use, and in these modern times that is very important.

The Metropolitan's line to Amersham north of Rickmansworth passes through some pleasant countryside which is far removed from the urban sprawl which builds up as the line gets closer to London. It can be strange to witness cricket being played on the village green, horses galloping across the common, and then the clatter of an Underground train rattling along in the background. This area is roughly 20 miles away from the centre of London and the pace of life here just seems that little bit slower. This view shows Chorleywood station with an Amersham to Baker Street service arriving on the 14th September 2008. This section of line is also served by diesel multiple unit trains which run between London Marylebone and Aylesbury and are operated by Chiltern Trains. To work on this line, the Chiltern Trains DMUs are fitted with the standard London Underground trip cocks.

While most A stock trains remained looking smart to the end of their working lives, a small number developed a rather shabby appearance in their latter days. This was especially the case with the front end of driving motor 5034 which took on a rather white pasty look, no doubt the result of removing unwanted graffiti. Here we see the train arriving into platform 3 at Harrow on the Hill with a train for Watford on the 24th March 2012. This set was used for the 'Farewell to A Stock' railtour on the 29th September 2012, and thankfully, the red end of 5034 was repainted for the occasion.

The track in platform 2 is of interest here, as this is the limit of London Underground operations with appropriate signage at the platform end, and the conductor rails coming to an abrupt halt just yards from the platform end. South of here, this track becomes the up Chiltern Line and is usually used only by the diesel multiple units operated by Chiltern Trains.

A busy scene at the London end of Wembley Park station as a train of A stock led by 5105 arrives with a service for Uxbridge. In the background is a northbound train of Jubilee Line 1996 stock, and beyond that another train of A stock is heading towards London. Immediately above the third coach of the approaching A stock can be seen the fly-under to Neasden Depot. This is the main depot of the Metropolitan Line, but is also used by the Jubilee Line to stable a small number of trains. The fly-under can be used by trains on both the Metropolitan and Jubilee Lines.

Clearly visible on this photo is the driver's window which is smaller than the window on the opposite side. However, a black rectangle has been painted underneath the window to make the two windows appear the same size. Originally the two large front windows were the same size but when the A stock trains were converted to One Person Operation, a row of buttons was installed on top of the driver's control desk which necessitated the fitting of a smaller window.

South of Wembley Park, Metropolitan trains run non stop on the fast lines as far as Finchley Road. The stations along this section of line being served only by trains on the Jubilee Line. One such station is Dollis Hill, from where this photograph has been taken against the backdrop of the Wembley Stadium arch. A train of A stock led by 5199 is approaching with an Amersham to Baker Street service. It is worth noting that the destination blind is showing 'Fast Baker Street' meaning that this train has run on the fast lines non-stop between Moor Park and Harrow on the Hill and between Harrow on the Hill and Wembley Park. This photo was taken on the 26th November 2011 when there were regular fast trains on the Metropolitan, but from December 2011, these were reduced to only run southbound in the morning peak, and northbound in the evening peak. It is not uncommon however, to occasionally still find trains running fast during the off peak especially if the train has been delayed on an earlier working and needs to regain some time.

Above: A train of A stock races past Kilburn Jubilee Line station with a service for Baker Street on the 27th March 2012. Nearing the end of its career, driving motor 5151 is looking a little neglected. Kilburn station was opened as Kilburn and Brondesbury in November 1879 by the Metropolitan Railway. It was served by the Metropolitan until services on the Stanmore branch were taken over by the Bakerloo in November 1939, and it was then served by the Bakerloo until the Stanmore branch was changed over to the Jubilee Line. Like the previous picture at Dollis Hill, only Jubilee Line trains call here, with all Metropolitan Line trains passing through non stop on the fast lines situated on the outside of the two Jubilee tracks.

Below: West Hampstead station is yet another station served only by the Jubilee with the Metropolitan Line tracks running on the outside of the Jubilee tracks. The station has a similar history to Kilburn, but was opened a few months earlier in June 1879 when it served as the temporary terminus of the Metropolitan Railway prior to the line being further extended to Willesden Green. Here we see a much smarter looking train of A stock led by 5189 passing through the station with a service for Baker Street on the 26th May 2012.

The new S stock trains which have replaced the A stock on the Met were built by Bombardier in Derby. Once built, the new trains have to be tested. The intensity of service makes it undesirable to carry out these tests on the London Underground, so before being delivered to Neasden Depot, the new trains are taken to the Old Dalby test track in Leicestershire to be tested. To get the trains to Old Dalby, they are hauled by diesel traction, usually Class 20s. On the 9th August 2011, S stock set 21051-21052 is being taken to Old Dalby in train 8X23 with 20301 at the far end hauling the train, and 20305 nearest the camera bringing up the rear. The train is passing Thurmaston on the slow line to the north of Leicester. The above train formation is unusual as the S stock moves usually have a pair of class 20s at each end. However on this occasion, due to the lack of available locos, a single engine at each end had to suffice, and this necessitated the use of the yellow wagons as additional brake force. The standard network rail air brakes are not compatible with the braking system on the S stock, so the S stock train is unbraked when being hauled, hence the need for the right amount of brake force in the rest of the train consist.

Once delivered to the Asfordby Test Centre on the Old Dalby test facility, the S stock trains are put through their paces on a 2.5 mile stretch north of Old Dalby, where the former up line has been fitted with the standard London Underground conductor rails. This image is taken close to the village of Upper Broughton and shows set 21062-21061 heading south at speed during a mileage accumulation run. The Old Dalby test track was once part of the Nottingham to London via Melton Mowbray and Corby main line and has been used to test many trains over the years, most notably the Advanced Passenger Train (APT). More recently, the Virgin 'Pendolino' trains were tested here and for this reason, both the up and the down lines have been fitted with 25kV ac overhead power lines. This will probably be the only occasion the S stock trains will be seen running under the wires.

Above: Once everything has been thoroughly tested on the Old Dalby test track, the Class 20s are used to haul the trains down to Neasden Depot on the Metropolitan Line. Here we see 20304 and 20301 hauling set 21033-21034 through East Goscote in Leicestershire on the 14th December 2011. The use of two locomotives at each end means the yellow box wagons used for additional brake force in the earlier photograph are not needed. With the couplings on the S stock being incompatible with the standard screw couplings on the class 20s, there is a barrier vehicle at each end of the train. These are converted from former oil tank wagons and have a standard screw coupling at one end, and a London Underground coupling at the other. The locomotives hauling this train are owned by Direct Rail Services, but as they are on hire to GB Railfreight, who operate the S stock moves, all DRS branding has been removed. Class 20s have to be used on these workings due to a weight restriction on the north end of the Metropolitan Line.

Below: Early in 2012, the Class 20s on hire from Direct Rail Services were returned to their owners and GB Railfreight began using alternative motive power for the S stock moves. These have come from various sources, and the two locos at the far end of the train, 20901 and 20905 are on hire from the Harry Needle Railroad Company, but the two locos on the front are preserved examples and carry retro liveries. Leading the train is 20227 in Railfreight Grey livery. This loco is owned by the Class Twenty Locomotive Society based at the Midland Railway Centre. The second loco is 20142 in BR Blue livery which is privately owned. On the 26th March 2012, train 7X09 the 1142 Old Dalby to Amersham approaches Wychnor Junction with set 21089-21090 in tow. Although the train is shown in schedules as Old Dalby to Amersham, the train actually runs from Asfordby Test Centre to Neasden Depot, Old Dalby being the nearest reporting point to Asfordby, and Amersham being the boundary between Network Rail and London Underground.

Above: As each new train arrived at Neasden Depot, it usually took three to four days to get the trains fit for service. As each new train of S stock entered service, a train of the old A stock would be withdrawn and sent away to be scrapped. The transition of the Metropolitan Line was rapid and after the first few trains had arrived, deliveries became more frequent and the old A stock was wiped out in just over a year. Here we see set 21074-21073 leaving Rayners Lane with an Uxbridge to Aldgate service on the 24th March 2012. The station buildings here are typical of those designed by Charles Holden in the 1930s with the main station building being a brick box with a reinforced flat concrete roof. Rayners Lane is a busy station shared between the Metropolitan Line and the Piccadilly Line. At the east end of the station just beyond the main building, Metropolitan Line trains turn left towards Harrow on the Hill while Piccadilly Line trains turn right towards Acton Town.

Below: The interior of an S stock train is vastly different to anything currently in service on the Underground. All trains up until this point consisted of individual carriages. Although there are doors between each carriage, these are for emergency use only and it is not possible to walk through the length of the train. The S stock however, is completely open from end to end and passengers can walk through the entire length of the train. This not only eases passenger flow, but also creates additional standing space where the carriages join. Some passengers will miss the A stock they have replaced though, as there are less seats and more standing room on the new trains.

Immediately to the south of Harrow on the Hill station, a track branches off the Metropolitan northbound fast line and crosses over the up Chiltern Line to join the down Chiltern line to enter platform 1. As seen in an earlier image, the conductor rails on the up Chiltern Line end in platform 2 of Harrow on the Hill station. South of here, the Metropolitan Line and the Chiltern Line of Network Rail become independent of each other, although they do run side by side all the way to Finchley Road. On the 26th May 2012, 21070-21069 approach Harrow on the Hill on the slow line with a northbound service heading for Watford. Harrow on the Hill is the hub of the Metropolitan Line and is where the Uxbridge branch diverges away from the lines to Watford, Chesham and Amersham.

North of Harrow on the Hill station, and the track layout now consists of six tracks. The track on the right is used mainly by mainline trains between Marylebone and Aylesbury, although this can also be used by Metropolitan trains heading for the fast lines to the north of Harrow. The second track in from the right is used by southbound mainline trains running between Aylesbury and Marylebone and also occasionally by Metropolitan trains terminating at Harrow from the north. The third track in is for Metropolitan trains heading north to either Watford, Chesham or Amersham, and the line on which S stock set 21094-21093 is seen is the line to Uxbridge which will shortly burrow down and under the other lines to emerge close to West Harrow station. The two tracks on the left of the photo are the southbound line from Uxbridge, and the southbound line from Watford, Chesham and Amersham.

On the evening of the 26th November 2011, S stock set 21008-21009 arrives at Wembley Park with a Baker Street to Uxbridge service. The top speed of the S stock trains is 62mph. This is faster than the A stock they replaced on the Metropolitan, but only because the A stock trains had their top speed reduced from 70mph to 50mph in the late 1990s to improve their reliability. A total of 58 trains of S stock were ordered for the Metropolitan Line, and these are all 8 car trains designated as S8.

Wembley Park station opened in October 1893, although Metropolitan Railway trains had been running through here since 1880. The station can become extremely busy whenever there is an event or a football match on at Wembley Stadium as the stadium is only a five minute walk from the station.

The wide formation to the west of West Hampstead station is photographed from the West End Lane overbridge opposite the entrance to the station. There is much to observe in this photograph with the two tracks of the Network Rail lines in and out of Marylebone on the extreme left of the picture, the northbound Metropolitan Line and then the northbound Jubilee Line on which a train of 1996 tube stock can be seen heading north and climbing up a steady gradient in order to cross over the top of the North London Line. In the centre of the picture is the reversing siding used to turn back some northbound Jubilee Line trains. Note the central position of the points here which would prevent a runaway train from this siding from reaching either of the adjacent running lines. The next track is the southbound Jubilee Line, and finally, the track on which our main subject, S stock set 21085-21086 is seen, is the southbound Metropolitan Line. The S stock set is working a southbound train to Baker Street on the 26th May 2012.

HAMMERSMITH & CITY LINE →

The Hammersmith & City Line currently runs between Hammersmith and Barking. The line to Hammersmith began life as a joint venture between the Great Western Railway and the Metropolitan Railway and was opened in 1864, although the current Hammersmith terminus did not open until 1868. The line runs at roof top level for the first part of the journey from Hammersmith, then, after passing through the H&C platforms alongside the main Paddington station, the line joins the northern side of the Circle Line at Praed Street Junction. The section of line from Paddington (Bishops Road) to Farringdon was the world's first underground railway and was opened by the Metropolitan Railway in January 1863. Hammersmith & City services follow this route through Edgware Road, Baker Street, Kings Cross & St Pancras to Farringdon and beyond through Moorgate and Liverpool Street to Aldgate Junction where they diverge left to join up with the District Line at Aldgate East. From here the H&C services compliment those on the District Line as far as Barking where the H&C trains terminate in a bay platform with the District Line continuing on to Upminster.

Until 1988, the H&C was shown on maps as part of the Metropolitan Line, but has since been shown separately and from 1990 was given its own colour of pink. Hammersmith & City Line trains are currently worked by trains of C stock introduced in two batches in 1969/70 (C69 stock) and 1977 (C77 stock), and also used on the Circle Line and the Wimbledon to Edgware Road route of the District Line. The days of the C stock trains are numbered as new 7 car trains of S stock are being introduced to replace them.

Above: A train of C77 stock arrives at Baker Street with a Hammersmith to Moorgate service on the 21st August 2010. Judging by the red reflections in the front window of the train, the signal for the road ahead is at danger. This is quite common here as just in front of the train is Baker Street Junction where the Metropolitan Line diverges and any trains coming off or going onto the Met will conflict with eastbound trains on the Hammersmith & City and Circle Lines. Of all the stations on the original section of the Metropolitan Railway, Baker Street retains its original character more than most. The overall brick arch is unaltered, and the wall ventilation recesses, although now blocked off, have been restored with lighting which makes it appear daylight is streaming in as it did when the station was built. The original trains were steam, and these vents were as much to let steam out as they were to let daylight in.

All is very quiet at the Hammersmith terminus of the Hammersmith & City Line on the morning of the 11th January 2012. The empty platforms are deceiving however, as this photograph was taken at the start of the morning rush hour, and the headlights of the train approaching in the distance signal that the peace will soon be shattered as a train load of commuters will fill the platform on the right. A train of C stock with 5539 at the rear is waiting its turn to depart towards Central London. Although the Metropolitan Railway's line to Hammersmith opened in June 1864, the original station was situated just north of here, with this station not being opened until December 1868. Hammersmith has two stations on the Underground, this one serving the Hammersmith & City and Circle lines, and another serving the District and Piccadilly lines. Although the two stations are just yards apart, there is no physical connection between the two.

Time is running out for the C stock in this view taken at Shepherd's Bush Market on the 11th January 2012. Although at the time of this photograph there were none of the new S stock trains in service, there were two trains based at Hammersmith Depot for overnight testing and driver familiarisation. There is also evidence of the changes being made to accommodate the new trains with the new platform extensions and S7 stop board already in place. By the start of 2013, the first few trains of S stock had entered service on the Hammersmith & City, although the C stock was still working the vast majority of services.

Here we see a train of C stock with 5511 at the rear departing with a Hammersmith to Barking service. Dominating the background of this picture are the Shepherd's Bush studios of the BBC, more commonly known as Television Centre. Shepherd's Bush Market station was called just Shepherd's Bush until 2008 when it was renamed to avoid confusion with the new Shepherd's Bush station on the West London Line, which also interchanges with the Central Line station of the same name.

Above: Moorgate sub surface station serves the Hammersmith & City, Circle and Metropolitan Lines. Most trains call at the two main through platforms, but there are also two bay platforms that can be used for terminating trains from the west. On the 21st August 2010, a weekend line closure east of Moorgate saw all Hammersmith & City trains terminate in the bay platforms, and here we see a train of C stock led by 5580 shortly after arrival with a service from Hammersmith. There are two further bay platforms visible to the left of the train. These are the former 'City Widened Lines' latterly used by Thameslink trains to and from Bedford. Those trains ceased running in December 2009 and these two platforms at Moorgate are now disused.

Below: At the west end of Liverpool Street station there is a remarkable survivor, a Metropolitan Railway signalbox. It closed as a signalbox as long ago as November 1956, but has seen further use as a relay room, which explains its survival. In this picture taken on the 23rd June 2012, it is being passed by a Hammersmith to Barking service formed of a train of C stock led by 5558. The west end of Liverpool Street station is very difficult to photograph with the sun lighting the scene, and this view was taken in the middle of summer towards the middle of the day when the sun was at its highest. On the left of the shot, there is yet another building under construction which will add even more shadows to the scene as it climbs ever higher. It is being built on what was once a third platform used for turning back trains from the west.

CIRCLE LINE →

Circle line services started in 1884, and until December 2009, it was an orbital Underground line which had a circular route around the centre of London with trains running either clockwise or counter clockwise around London. From 2009, the route of the Circle was extended to include the Hammersmith branch from Praed Street Junction. Circle Line trains running from Hammersmith usually have the eventual destination of Edgware Road, and run to Praed Street Junction where they join the original Circle. They then pass through Edgware Road and continue round the circle in a clockwise direction to Edgware Road, where they reverse and head back round the Circle in a counter clockwise direction, through Edgware Road yet again and back to Hammersmith. The Circle is the only sub surface line which shares tracks with all of the other sub surface lines, the Metropolitan from Baker Street Junction to Aldgate, the Hammersmith & City from Hammersmith to Aldgate Junction and the District from Minories Junction to Gloucester Road and High Street Kensington to Edgware Road. Like the Hammersmith & City Line, trains are formed of C stock, which are gradually being phased out by new trains of S stock. There are stations on the Circle which can only accommodate 6 car trains of C stock, so the longer trains of S stock will make use of selective door opening at some stations, with any door not lined up with the platform remaining closed. To do this with older stock would have caused a problem, as passengers cannot walk through to the next carriage to alight. The S stock trains by contrast have an open plan interior, so passengers can walk through the train to the next available opening door.

Above: When the Circle Line began operating trains to Hammersmith, the line between Paddington and Hammersmith didn't see much change other than a more frequent service and selected trains showing Circle Line on their destination blind, the trains used on the Circle being of the same type as those already used on the Hammersmith and City Line. This is Latimer Road and a train of C stock has just departed towards Paddington and the centre of London with a Hammersmith to Edgware Road Circle Line service on the 11th January 2012.

One of the later build of C stock built in 1977 (known as C77 stock) pauses at Euston Square with an outer rail (clockwise) Circle Line service on the 15th February 2011. The long straight platforms here mean a simple mirror is all that is needed for the driver to look back along his train when closing the doors, and this mirror can be seen suspended from the ceiling to the right of the train. The longer trains of the Metropolitan Line which also serve this station pull up at a second mirror further along the platform. Euston Square station serves the Hammersmith & City Line, Circle Line and Metropolitan Line, and despite its modern appearance, its history goes back to 1863 when it opened as Gower Street as part of the Metropolitan Railway's Paddington to Farringdon line. The station's name was changed to Euston Square in 1909.

Barbican station lies between Moorgate and Kings Cross on the Hammersmith & City, Circle and Metropolitan Lines. The station was originally called Aldersgate Street, but after several subtle name changes over the years, became Barbican in 1968. In this view, a Circle Line train formed of C stock is calling at the eastbound platform while working a Hammersmith to Edgware Road service on the 23rd June 2012. Of note are the remains of the wall brackets on the retaining walls on either side of the station. These used to be part of an overall glass roof which was shattered during a World War II air raid in December 1941.

On the right of the photo are the abandoned and weed strewn tracks of the City Widened Lines. This section of line was latterly operated as part of the Thameslink network with trains running between Bedford and Moorgate. However, the core Thameslink services were running through to the former Southern Region by turning right at Farringdon and running through the Snow Hill Tunnel, and in order to increase the length of these trains to 12 carriages, the platforms at Farringdon were extended across the junction, thus blocking the line to Moorgate. This forced the closure of the City Widened Lines beyond Farringdon, and the last trains ran in December 2009. Although only latterly served by trains from the Midland main line, the City Widened Lines were also served by trains from the Great Northern main line until they were diverted at Finsbury Park to serve Moorgate via the Northern City Line instead.

DISTRICT LINE →

Like the other Sub surface lines, the District will also have its current fleet of trains replaced by new S stock trains, however, the District will be the last to receive the new trains as the D stock trains on the District were the newest sub surface trains on the Underground prior to the introduction of the S stock. The D stock was built by Metro-Cammell in Birmingham and first entered service in January 1980 with the entire fleet delivered by 1983. As well as the D stock, the District also uses several trains of C stock on the Wimbledon to Edgware Road service which runs up the west side of the Circle Line where the platforms are too short to accommodate the longer D stock.

The District Line began life as the Metropolitan District Railway (more commonly known as the District Railway), with the first section opening between South Kensington and Westminster in 1868. Later extensions took the District Railway to Uxbridge (1910), Hounslow Barracks (1886), Ealing Broadway (1879), Richmond (1877), Wimbledon (1889), Addisson Road, now Kensington Olympia (1872) and Upminster (1902). All of these branches are still part of the District Line except the Uxbridge and Hounslow Barracks (now named Hounslow West) branches, which have been transferred to the Piccadilly.

Above: A line up of trains out of service in daylight hours is rare and is usually the result of line closures for planned engineering works. This photo is no exception and was taken on a day when the east end of the District Line between Tower Hill and Upminster was closed for track relaying. This is a line up of D stock in the stabling roads at Upminster Depot on the 29th August 2009, with the lowest numbered vehicle 7000 nearest the camera.

D stock driving motor 7094 pokes out of the Heavy Lifting Shop at Upminster depot on the 29th August 2009. Upminster is the main depot for the District Line and is situated beyond the station where District Line services from the west terminate. In fact, the depot is the eastern most extremity of the entire London Underground network. The depot is responsible, along with Ealing Common depot, for maintaining the District's fleet of D stock. Along with a handful of C stock trains, the D stock have dominated District Line services since the early 1980s, but present plans should see them all replaced by the S stock by 2016.

Above: Aldgate East station lies at the east side of the Aldgate triangle. At the west end of the station is Aldgate East Junction where the District Line turns left to join the southern side of the Circle at Minories Junction, and the Hammersmith & City Line turns right to join the northern side of the Circle at Aldgate Junction. On the third side of this triangle between Aldgate Junction and Minories Junction is Aldgate station which is served by trains on the Circle Line as well as by trains on the Metropolitan Line which terminate in the bay platforms there. This photo shows a train of D stock waiting to depart from Aldgate East station with a Whitechapel to Ealing Broadway service on the 18th July 2010. The current station here was opened in October 1938 and replaced the original Aldgate East station that lay a few hundred yards further west. The station had to be re-sited when the triangle junction was enlarged as part of the 1930s New Works Programme.

Below: Gloucester Road sub surface station was opened by the Metropolitan Railway in October 1868 as Brompton (Gloucester Road) when it was the temporary terminus of the Metropolitan Railway line from Paddington Praed Street. In December of the same year, the MR extended the line to South Kensington where it joined up with the Metropolitan District Railway's line from South Kensington to Westminster which opened on the same day. Today, Gloucester Road is served by trains on the District and Circle Lines at sub surface level, and also below ground by the deep level tube station of the Piccadilly which was opened by the Great Northern, Piccadilly & Brompton Railway in 1906. Until the 1990s, the sub surface platforms were in the open air, but a raft was built over the station and a shopping mall and apartments built over the top. Here we see a train of D stock arriving with a service for Richmond on the 21st February 2009.

The bulk of services on the District are operated by 6 car trains of D stock. However, the Wimbledon to Edgware Road service is operated by C stock trains, which although still 6 cars in length, have a much shorter overall length than the D stock trains. After leaving Earls Court, District trains heading for Edgware Road run on the west side of the Circle Line where the stations at High Street Kensington, Notting Hill Gate, Bayswater, Paddington and Edgware Road are all too short to accommodate the longer D stock, although there are two bay platforms at High Street Kensington which are long enough to be used by terminating trains of D stock. When the new trains of 7 car S stock take over these services, there will be a number of doors outside the station platform which will not open, but as the new trains are open plan inside, passengers will be able to quickly move to the nearest available door which does open.

This picture shows a train of C stock departing from Notting Hill Gate with an Edgware Road to Wimbledon service on the 21st January 2012. Notting Hill Gate station was opened by the Metropolitan Railway in October 1868 and to this day still retains many original features including the impressive overall roof. Interchange with the Central Line is also available here.

Above: The Wimbledon branch of the District sees a mix of C stock and D stock working services. Those travelling between Wimbledon and Edgware Road must be formed of the shorter C stock as already mentioned, but D stock can still be used on services between Wimbledon and other destinations. Here a train of C stock arrives at Putney Bridge with an Edgware Road to Wimbledon service on the 10th July 2010. The train is using the outer through platform here, the middle platform being a dead end used for turning back trains. However, this middle road is not long enough to accommodate a train of D stock, so only trains of C stock can turn back here. Putney Bridge was opened as Putney Bridge & Fulham by the Metropolitan & District Railway in March 1880. It was the terminus of the line until 1889 when the Fulham Railway Bridge over the River Thames was opened and the line extended to East Putney, where it connected to the London & South Western Railway's line to Wimbledon. The station changed its name to Putney Bridge & Hurlingham in 1902 and then became just Putney Bridge thirty years later. Despite the name, Putney Bridge station is in Fulham, Putney being on the opposite side of the River Thames.

Below: Further along the Wimbledon branch, and a train of D stock heads for Wimbledon and is captured approaching Wimbledon Park station on the 10th July 2010. This section of line was opened by the LSWR in 1889 with the Metropolitan District Railway operating its trains over the route to reach Wimbledon. The LSWR (and later the Southern Railway) also operated trains over this line as far as East Putney where they branched off to join the Clapham Junction to Barnes line. These services ended in 1941, but main line trains still use the line to run empty to and from Wimbledon depot. The line was part of British Rail until 1994 when it was transferred into London Underground ownership.

All branches of the District meet at Earls Court making this a very busy station, and it is rare during the day to see all of the four platforms empty. The branches from Ealing Broadway, Kensington Olympia, Richmond and Wimbledon all converge on the west end of the station, with the Edgware Road route and the main arm of the District to Upminster converging on the east end. In this view, a train of C stock is arriving from the west with a train for High Street Kensington on the 19th June 2011.

Earls Court station not only has the four platforms on the District underneath the impressive overall roof, but there are also two platforms underground serving the Piccadilly Line, making this a very important interchange between the two lines.

Led by 7539, an unpainted aluminum train of D stock arrives at Ealing Common with an Ealing Broadway to Tower Hill service on the 16th September 2007. Ever since the 1950s, new trains on the London Underground have been made from aluminium, and the trains ran with little or no paint on the exterior surfaces giving them a silver appearance. By the 1990s the Underground was suffering badly at the hands of graffiti vandals, and the plain silver trains became a natural target. While the unwanted graffiti could be removed with chemicals, it left a shadow of the graffiti etched into the aluminium, and the London Underground took the decision to paint all trains in a smart red, white and blue livery which not only looked better, but was also a little more resilient to having graffiti cleaned off it. The last line to run with unpainted aluminium trains was the District, and the final silver train was removed from service for repainting and refurbishment in February 2008, just a few months after this photograph was taken.

Engineering Trains

It is not unusual for early morning commuters to be faced with sights such as this. With only a few hours during the night when the Underground is shut down, a number of engineering trains descend on the system to perform a whole host of repair and maintenance tasks. These trains are often still making their way back to depot when the service begins again in the morning. Here we see battery loco L18 at the head of a train as it passes through Rayners Lane station with a train heading back to Ruislip Depot on the 11th January 2012. Most engineering trains work out of either Ruislip or Lillie Bridge depots and mostly use battery locos, usually one at each end of the train. These locos can operate using the traction current picked up from the conductor rails, or from on board batteries when they are operating in areas where the traction current has been turned off.

Although battery locos spend most of their lives working at night or during line closures at weekends, it is sometimes possible to see them during the daytime running between normal service trains, although due to the intensity of the service on most lines, they are fairly rare during the day. This is one such occasion, the 11th January 2012, and this is train 646 the 1138 Hammersmith Depot to Ruislip Depot. L52 leads the train in the distance with L50 bringing up the rear as the train passes through Latimer Road station. Both L50 and L52 were part of a batch of locomotives built by BREL at Doncaster between 1973 and 1974.

At the time of this photograph, Hammersmith Depot was being upgraded ready for the introduction of the new S stock trains, and due to the narrow nature of the streets surrounding the depot, the only way to remove the spoil was by rail, and this working ran on a number of occasions.

Besides the battery locomotives, the London Underground has a variety of trains which have been adapted or modified from old stock to perform specific tasks. This is one of two trains of former Central Line 1962 stock trains which have been converted into Rail Adhesion Trains for use during the autumn leaf fall season. One is used at the east end of the line, where the Central Line runs through part of the Epping Forest, while the other train sees use between Ruislip, North Acton and Ealing Broadway. Although often joked about by the national press, leaves on the line are a problem for any railway, causing trains to slip when accelerating and skid while trying to stop. The Rail Adhesion Trains apply a sticky paste known as Sandite to the rail which assists with adhesion. This scene shows the east end train running as train 488, the 13:28 Hainault Depot - Leytonstone - Epping - Woodford - Newbury Park - Hainault Depot. The train is departing Woodford on the leg to Newbury Park. The 1962 stock was once a common sight on the Central Line, as they operated the bulk of services between 1962 and 1995 when they were replaced by the 1992 stock.

Heritage Trains

Locomotive number 12 'Sarah Siddons' of 1923 is one of two surviving electric locomotives built by the Metropolitan Vickers Company in Barrow in Furness for the Metropolitan Railway. There were twenty locos built and they were used on services between London and Aylesbury as far as Rickmansworth which was as far as the electrification reached at the time, and from where steam traction took over for the remainder of the journey. When the line north of Rickmansworth was electrified to Chesham and Amersham in the early 1960s, the locos were replaced by the A stock trains, as per the train on the left. In this view, number 12 is bringing up the rear of an Amersham to Harrow on the Hill special as it approaches its destination. Meanwhile, a train of A stock led by 5227 is departing towards Uxbridge. 14th September 2008.

Normally based at the London Transport Museum's Acton Depot adjacent to Ealing Common Depot, the four car set of 1938 stock owned by the London Transport Museum is occasionally used on special excursions around the London Underground network. With vehicle 11012 nearest the camera, the train has just arrived at Ealing Common station from depot ready to work an enthusiast's tour to Charing Cross on the Jubilee Line on the 16th September 2007.

The 1938 stock was built by Metropolitan Cammell and the Birmingham Railway Carriage and Wagon Company and served the London Underground for fifty years between 1938 and 1988. They were used on the Bakerloo, Northern, Piccadilly, East London and Central Lines during their careers. Only the set in this photograph still sees passenger use on the London Underground, but several vehicles were sold on to British Rail Network Southeast for further employment on the Isle of Wight, where they can still be seen in daily use.

A scene which was at one time so common, a train of 1938 tube stock on the Piccadilly Line. This is the 21st June 2009, and the LT Museum's 1938 stock train had spent the day working tours over the Northern Line. In order to get the train back home to Acton Depot, the final run involved crossing from the Northern to the Piccadilly at Kings Cross & St Pancras and then running via the Piccadilly to Ealing Common via Ealing Broadway. This run is seen passing through the westbound Piccadilly Line platform at Gloucester Road. Unfortunately, as Underground lines are upgraded and new signalling and automatic train operation is introduced, the sphere of operation for this popular little train is shrinking. It can no longer operate on the Central and Jubilee Lines and never has been able to operate over the Victoria Line.

If you wish to sample the delights of the old 1938 tube stock on a daily basis, then you need look no further than the Isle of Wight. A height restriction in Ryde tunnel means that standard height trains cannot be used, and when the line between Ryde Pier Head and Shanklin was electrified in 1967, British Rail purchased a fleet of pre-1938 standard tube stock trains from London Transport. In 1989, a decision was made to upgrade(!) the line's rolling stock by purchasing some 1938 tube stock recently withdrawn from the Northern Line of London Underground. The fifty year old 'new' trains entered service as two car sets in the very smart Network Southeast livery, and after a period carrying a rather colourful 'dinosaur' livery, now carry a livery close to their former London Transport red livery, spoilt only by the application of the standard British Rail / Network Rail yellow warning panel on the front. Here we see sets 483004 and 483008 emerging from Ryde tunnel and approaching Ryde Esplanade station with the 1617 Shanklin to Ryde Pier Head on the 27th July 2008.

It is not just the rolling stock which is second hand on the Isle of Wight. The sole remaining working signalbox on the line at Ryde St Johns Road is also second hand, having originally stood at Waterloo Junction in London. Built in 1901 by the South East & Chatham Railway, the box was moved to the island in 1926 and today controls the entire line from Ryde Pier Head to Shanklin. In this view taken on the 27th July 2008, the 08:17 Shanklin to Ryde Pier Head is entering Ryde St Johns Road station and is being worked by 483004 and 483008. It will be noted that the trains no longer run on the standard London Underground four rail system, having been converted to the standard BR Southern Region three rail system prior to being shipped to the island. Taking a ride on one of the Isle of Wight's trains of 1938 stock is pure magic. Despite being heavily refurbished, they still make all the same noises they did when they ran on the Underground. A Londoner could go for a ride, close their eyes, and easily imagine they were back home!

You've read the book... now see the movie!

LONDON UNDERGROUND DVDs

We have 26 London Underground titles:
Driver's Eye Views, documentaries and historical DVDs -
all available directly from Videoscene.

For full details of all these DVDs visit our website. In the left hand menu click on 'Underground and Tube' and details will appear.
We have more than 2,000 other railway and transport DVDs and Blu-rays available, visit www.videoscene.co.uk for full details.
Telephone 01253 738336 and ask for your **FREE catalogue**

The UK's Premier Railway DVD Retailer